MUDRAS FOR MENTAL HEALTH

Calm Your Thoughts, Achieve Mindfulness, Balance Emotions, and Awaken Your True Self

By

SHILPA MEHTA

Dedication

To my daughter Reekta, son-in-law Karan, and grandchildren, whose love and faith in me have been a constant source of strength and joy.

To my sister Trupti, Dr. Rohit Gandhi, and my friend Dr. Sanjivv Gandhi, whose unwavering love and encouragement have been invaluable.

This book is my humble offering to my late mother and Yogi Vinod, whose influence and guidance continue to inspire me.

Your support has made this work possible, and your spirit shines through every page.

Thank you for being a part of this journey and for helping to make this dream a reality.

SPECIAL THANKS

*Special thanks to **Ms. Renu Mathur** for her exceptional artwork, which has beautifully enhanced my books on chakras, meditation, and mudras, including this one, Mudras for Mental Health.*

Her creativity and attention to detail have beautifully brought these concepts to life, enhancing the reading and learning experience for all.

Her artistic vision has added a unique and meaningful touch to these works, and I am deeply grateful for her contribution.

TABLE OF CONTENTS

THE ROLE OF COMPLEMENTARY APPROACHES 9

THE INTERCONNECTEDNESS OF PHYSICAL AND MENTAL HEALTH 13

PANCHA MAHABHUTAS AND MENTAL HEALTH 21

PANCHA PRANAS AND MENTAL HEALTH 33

THE INTERRELATION BETWEEN GUT AND MENTAL HEALTH 43

MENTAL HEALTH AND ITS RELATION TO THE NERVOUS SYSTEM 51

IMPACT OF MENTAL HEALTH ON THE HEART 59

CONNECTION BETWEEN MENTAL HEALTH AND THE SKELETAL SYSTEM 67

RELATIONSHIP BETWEEN BODY WEIGHT, BODY IMAGE, AND MENTAL HEALTH 77

DISCLAIMER 89

ABOUT THE AUTHOR 91

MAY I ASK YOU FOR A SMALL FAVOR? 93

OTHER BOOKS FROM THE AUTHOR 95

THE ROLE OF COMPLEMENTARY APPROACHES

The Need for Holistic Approaches

Mental health disorders manifest not only as clinical symptoms but also as emotional, psychological, and social challenges. While conventional treatments are essential, they often focus primarily on symptom management rather than addressing the underlying causes of mental distress. This limitation is evident in high rates of relapse, treatment resistance, and the persistent stigma surrounding mental health care. Consequently, there is an urgent need for holistic approaches that consider the mind-body connection, emotional well-being, and spiritual health.

The statistics surrounding mental health disorders reveal that traditional medical approaches frequently fall short in addressing the complexities of these challenges. With one in five adults experiencing a mental illness every year, the prevalence of mental health issues highlights the necessity for a more comprehensive approach that transcends conventional therapies. This is where complementary practices like mudras come into play.

Holistic health emphasizes treating the whole person rather than merely isolated symptoms. By integrating practices such as mudras into mental health management, individuals can explore alternative avenues for healing and empowerment. This approach recognizes that mental health is influenced by a variety of factors, including lifestyle, environment, and emotional states—all of which can be addressed through complementary practices.

The Potential Benefits of Incorporating Mudras

Mudras, or symbolic hand gestures used in yoga and meditation, provide a simple yet powerful way to enhance mental well-being. Here are key benefits of incorporating mudras into mental health management:

Energy Flow and Emotional Balance

Mudras influence the body's energy flow, helping to balance the Pancha Pranas (five vital forces) and promote emotional stability. For instance, Gyan Mudra enhances mental clarity, while Shunya Mudra alleviates restlessness and anxiety.

Mindfulness and Stress Reduction

Practicing mudras encourages mindfulness, essential for reducing stress and anxiety. Focusing on hand positions and breathing cultivates present-moment awareness, helping to calm racing thoughts and emotional turmoil. Integrating mudras into daily routines offers moments of grounding amid daily chaos.

Accessibility and Ease of Practice

Mudras are highly accessible, requiring no special equipment and can be practiced anywhere. This makes them an ideal complement for those lacking access to traditional mental health resources, fitting seamlessly into busy schedules.

Empowerment and Self-Management

Incorporating mudras into mental health management empowers individuals to take an active role in their healing process, fostering a sense of agency and enhancing emotional resilience to navigate life's challenges more effectively.

Support for Traditional Treatments

While mudras are not a substitute for professional mental health care, they can significantly complement traditional treatments. When integrated into a comprehensive mental health plan, mudras enhance the effectiveness of therapies, medications, and counseling by addressing both physical and emotional aspects of well-being, facilitating deeper healing and promoting long-term health.

Conclusion

As mental health disorders rise, exploring holistic methods becomes crucial for supporting emotional and mental balance. Incorporating mudras into mental health management offers a powerful, accessible, and empowering tool that complements traditional therapies. This integrative approach fosters resilience and encourages individuals to take charge of their emotional well-being, cultivating a life of balance, peace, and clarity.

The Interconnectedness of Physical and Mental Health

Introduction

Traditional practices like yoga and Ayurveda have long emphasized that health is a blend of physical, mental, emotional, social, and spiritual well-being, all deeply interconnected. It's a holistic approach, where balance in all dimensions is key to true wellness.

In this chapter, we'll explore how these aspects work together to form the foundation for overall well-being, empowering us to make more integrated choices for lasting health.

Mental and emotional health are interconnected but distinct:

- **Mental Health**: Refers to overall psychological well-being, influencing how we think, feel, behave, handle stress, relate to others, and build resilience.

- **Emotional Health**: Focuses on understanding, expressing, and managing emotions constructively, embracing positive feelings like joy and gratitude, and navigating negative ones.

Mental health is broader, while emotional health zeroes in on managing emotions in daily life.

Now, let's explore the connections between these different aspects of health.

The Physical-Mental Health Connection

Physical and mental health are closely linked, each impacting the other:

- **Stress and the Body**: Chronic stress triggers hormones like cortisol, weakening immunity, raising blood pressure, and causing heart or digestive issues.

- **Depression and Fatigue**: Depression brings fatigue, aches, and insomnia, lowering energy and increasing illness risk.

- **Anxiety and Physical Symptoms**: Anxiety can cause rapid heart rate, dizziness, sweating, and digestive issues, often leading to chronic pain.

- **Mental Health and Chronic Illness**: Poor mental health worsens chronic conditions like diabetes and heart disease, creating a negative health cycle.

How Physical Health Affects Mental Health

- **Exercise and Mood**: Regular activity releases endorphins, reducing stress, enhancing sleep, and boosting self-esteem.

- **Nutrition and Brain Health**: A balanced diet supports brain function, while poor nutrition may cause anxiety and mood swings.

- **Chronic Pain and Mental Health**: Pain can lead to depression and frustration due to physical limitations.

- **Sleep and Cognitive Function**: Good sleep is vital for emotional balance, while lack of sleep worsens mental health.

The Emotional Health Connection

Emotional health is key to balancing mental and physical well-being by managing emotions effectively:

- **Impact on Mental Health**:

  - **Unresolved Emotions:** Suppressed feelings like anger or grief may lead to anxiety, depression, or emotional numbness.

- **Emotional Resilience:** Developing emotional intelligence and resilience helps tackle challenges and prevents burnout.

- **Impact on Physical Health**:

- **Physical Manifestations**: Emotions often show up as muscle tension, headaches, or fatigue.

- **Heart Health:** Emotional stress can trigger heart problems, such as "broken heart syndrome," mimicking heart attack symptoms.

The Spiritual Health Connection

Spiritual health fosters inner peace and a sense of purpose through practices like meditation, mindfulness, or prayer:

- **Impact on Mental Health**:

- **Sense of Purpose:** A clear purpose brings hope, protecting against depression.

- **Mindfulness and Meditation:** These reduce stress, anxiety, and depression while improving clarity and calm.

- **Impact on Physical Health**:

- **Stress Reduction:** Practices like prayer or meditation lower stress and the risk of related illnesses.

- **Immune Boost:** Spiritual practices enhance immunity, supporting recovery and illness prevention.

Social Health Connection

Social health, the quality of relationships, is vital to well-being. Strong connections promote support, while isolation harms mental and physical health.

- **Impact on Mental Health:**

  - **Support Systems:** A strong social network reduces loneliness and buffers against stress.

  - **Positive Interactions:** Healthy relationships improve mood and self-esteem.

- **Impact on Physical Health:**

  - **Loneliness and Physical Health:** Social isolation raises the risk of heart disease and premature death, while social support promotes recovery and longevity.

Holistic Health: The Balance of All Aspects

True well-being is achieved by balancing physical, mental, emotional, spiritual, and social health. Each dimension influences the others:

- **Physical health** supports mental clarity and emotional stability.

- **Mental health** helps us make better choices for physical and emotional well-being.

- **Emotional health** enables stress management and stronger relationships.

- **Spiritual health** gives purpose, anchoring mental and emotional well-being.

- **Social health** fosters connections, enhancing feelings of love and support.

By understanding these connections, we can take a more holistic approach, using tools like mudras, yoga, and mindfulness to promote overall health.

Conclusion

Holistic health thrives on balancing physical, mental, emotional, spiritual, and social dimensions. Neglecting one impacts the rest, highlighting the need for harmony.

True well-being starts with detoxifying the body and deconditioning the mind. By cleansing physical and mental toxicity, we create a foundation for healing. This journey involves practicing Prana Shuddhi and Bhuta Shuddhi, explored in the next chapters.

PANCHA MAHABHUTAS AND MENTAL HEALTH

In Yogic and Ayurvedic philosophy, the entire universe—including the human body and mind - is composed of five fundamental elements, known as the Pancha Mahabhutas: Earth (Prithvi), Water (Jala), Fire (Agni), Air (Vayu), and Ether (Akasha). These elements are the building blocks of all matter and energy and play a critical role in both physical and mental health.

Each of the Pancha Mahabhutas corresponds to specific mental qualities and emotions, and their balance is crucial for mental well-being. When one or more elements become imbalanced, it can manifest as mental or emotional disturbances, such as stress, anxiety, depression, or irritability. Understanding these elements and their impact on the mind helps create a more harmonious mental state.

The Five Elements and Mental Health

1. Earth (Prithvi)

The Earth element represents stability, groundedness, and structure. It is associated with strength, endurance, and physical and mental resilience.

Mental Connection: A strong Earth element provides a sense of stability, security, and calmness. It helps in grounding thoughts and emotions, making it easier to handle stress and maintain emotional balance.

Imbalance: When the Earth element is deficient, individuals may feel anxious, scattered, or insecure. They might experience a lack of focus, mental fatigue, or a sense of being ungrounded. An excess can cause stubbornness or mental rigidity.

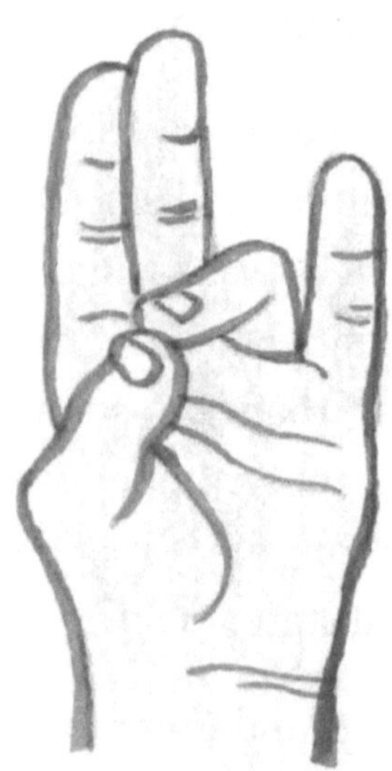

Forming the Mudra:

- Sit comfortably either on the floor or a chair, with your back straight and shoulders relaxed.

- Place your hands on your lap or thighs, palms facing up.

- Touch the tip of your ring finger (associated with the earth element) to the tip of your thumb, keeping the other three fingers extended straight.

- Maintain a calm and rhythmic breathing pattern throughout the practice.

Benefits: Prithvi Mudra (Earth Mudra) balances the Earth element and helps stabilize as well as ground the mind, promoting mental resilience and a sense of security.

2. Water (Jala)

The Water element governs fluidity, adaptability, and emotions. It is responsible for the smooth flow of thoughts and feelings and is deeply connected to emotional expression.

Mental Connection: Water provides emotional flexibility and the ability to adapt to changing circumstances. It fosters creativity, emotional clarity, and empathy.

Imbalance: A lack of Water can lead to emotional rigidity, difficulty in expressing feelings, and a sense of isolation. An excess of Water may cause emotional overwhelm, mood swings, or a tendency to be overly sensitive.

Forming the Mudra:

- Sit comfortably either on the floor or a chair, with your back straight and shoulders relaxed.

- Place your hands on your lap or thighs, palms facing up.

- Touch the tip of your little finger (which represents the water element) to the tip of your thumb, keeping the other three fingers extended straight.

- Maintain a calm and rhythmic breathing pattern throughout the practice.

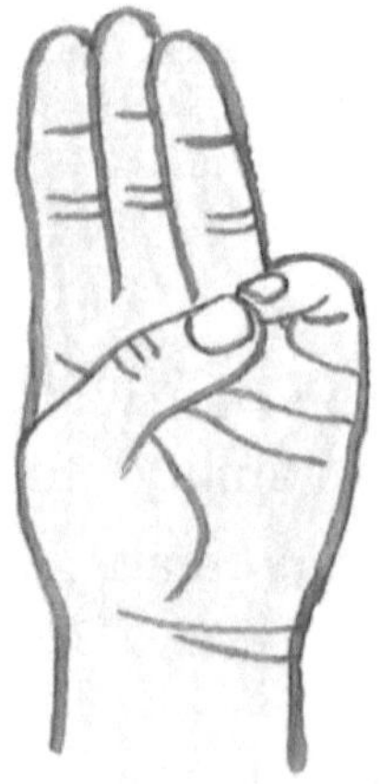

Benefits: Varun Mudra (Water Mudra) balances the Water element and helps restore emotional balance, enhance creativity, and promote emotional fluidity.

3. Fire (Agni)

The Fire element is associated with transformation, energy, and power. It governs passion, motivation, and mental clarity, and is responsible for digestion—both physical and mental (the assimilation of thoughts).

Mental Connection: Fire brings clarity, focus, and determination. It helps in processing emotions and thoughts, turning ideas into actions. When balanced, it fosters self-confidence, enthusiasm, and a sense of purpose.

Imbalance: A deficiency in Fire can result in lethargy, lack of motivation, or mental fog. An excess can lead to irritability, anger, or aggression.

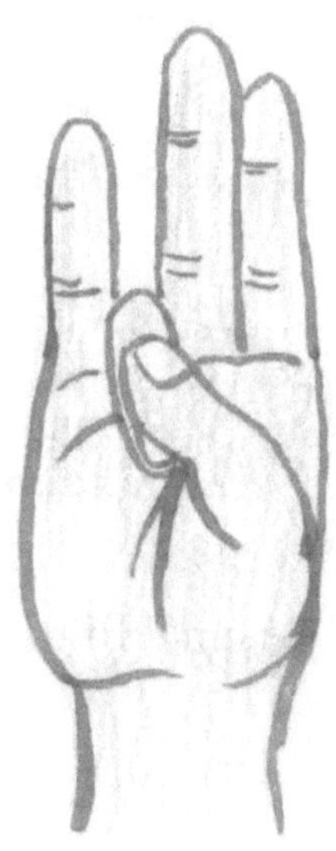

Forming the Mudra:

- Sit comfortably either on the floor or a chair, with your back straight and shoulders relaxed.

- Place your hands on your lap or thighs, palms facing up.

- Bend your ring finger and press its tip gently against the base of your thumb.

- Lightly press the thumb down on the bent ring finger while keeping the other three fingers extended straight.

- Maintain a calm and rhythmic breathing pattern throughout the practice.

Benefits: Surya Mudra (Sun Mudra) balances the Sun element helping ignite mental clarity, focus, and inner motivation while cooling excessive anger or irritability.

4. Air (Vayu)

The Air element represents movement, freedom, and communication. It governs thoughts, ideas, and intellectual activity, enabling mental agility and flexibility.

Mental Connection: Air supports creativity, adaptability, and clear communication. It enables the free flow of ideas and helps the mind stay open and receptive.

Imbalance: An imbalance of Air can result in scattered thoughts, anxiety, and mental restlessness. Too little Air can make the mind feel sluggish and stuck, while too much can create excessive mental chatter and worry.

Forming the Mudra:

- Sit comfortably either on the floor or a chair, with your back straight and shoulders relaxed.

- Place your hands on your lap or thighs, palms facing up.

- Bend your index finger and press it against the base of your thumb. Gently press the thumb on the bent index finger. Keep the other three fingers extended but relaxed.

- Maintain a calm and rhythmic breathing pattern throughout the practice.

Benefits: Mudra (Air Mudra) balances the Air element promoting calmness of the mind, reducing anxiety, and promoting mental clarity and focus.

5. Ether (Akasha)

The Ether element, or space, is the most subtle of the Pancha Mahabhutas. It represents expansiveness, openness, and awareness. It governs the mind's connection to higher consciousness and spiritual growth.

Mental Connection: Ether provides a sense of inner spaciousness and peace. It allows for self-reflection, spiritual awareness, and connection to higher wisdom. It encourages mental openness and creativity.

Imbalance: When Ether is out of balance, individuals may feel disconnected, lonely, or lost. A deficiency may result in a lack of imagination or difficulty accessing higher thoughts, while excess Ether can lead to overthinking or detachment from reality.

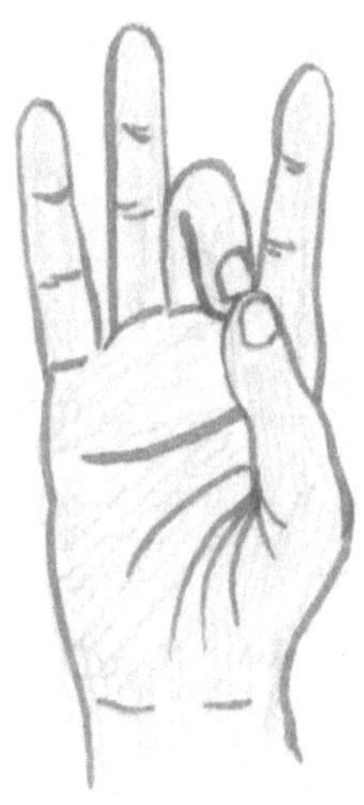

Forming the Mudra:

- Sit comfortably either on the floor or a chair, with your back straight and shoulders relaxed.

- Place your hands on your lap or thighs, palms facing up.

- Touch the tip of your middle finger to the tip of your thumb.

- Keep the other three fingers extended straight, ensuring your hands remain relaxed.

- Maintain a calm and rhythmic breathing pattern throughout the practice.

Benefits: Akasha Mudra (Space Mudra) balances the Space element promoting mental clarity, intuition, and a sense of inner peace by creating space in the mind.

Mudras to Balance the Pancha Mahabhutas for Mental Health:

By incorporating mudras that target the five elements, we can balance the energetic forces that impact both our physical and mental states. Each mudra directs energy in specific ways, aligning the elemental forces and bringing harmony to the mind and emotions.

For mental health, focusing on balancing these elements can help manage anxiety, stress, depression, and other emotional disturbances. Some commonly recommended mudras for balancing the elements include:

- Prithvi Mudra (Earth): For grounding and stability.

- Varun Mudra (Water): For emotional fluidity and calmness.

- Surya Mudra (Fire): For motivation, clarity, and transformation.

- Vayu Mudra (Air): For reducing anxiety and calming the mind.

- Akasha Mudra (Ether): For enhancing inner peace and spiritual connection.

Conclusion:

The Pancha Mahabhutas are the foundation of both our physical and mental health. By understanding the role that each element plays in our emotional and mental well-being, we can use simple yet powerful practices like mudras to bring balance and harmony to our lives. Balancing these elements helps in achieving a state of mental clarity, emotional stability, and inner peace, creating a holistic path to mental wellness. Through the wisdom of these ancient practices, we can learn to navigate the challenges of modern life with greater grace and resilience.

Pancha Pranas and Mental Health

In yogic philosophy, the human body is sustained by five vital life forces, known as the Pancha Pranas. These pranas are responsible for the functioning of both the physical body and the subtle, energetic layers. The five pranas are Prana, Apana, Samana, Udana, and Vyana. There are five sub or Upapranas too. They are extensions of the five main pranas (Prana, Apana, Vyana, Udana, and Samana) that govern specific physiological functions. These five sub-pranas are:

1. **Naga** – Governs burping and belching, responsible for expelling air from the stomach.

2. **Kurma** – Controls the blinking of the eyes and sharpens vision.

3. **Krikara** – Governs sneezing, as well as hunger and thirst.

4. **Devadatta** – Responsible for yawning and the urge to sleep.

5. **Dhananjaya** – Associated with bodily decomposition after death and certain functions like digestion and heart-related activities during life.

These sub-pranas regulate minor yet vital activities, complementing the roles of the main pranas in maintaining the body's balance.

Together, they govern all aspects of our existence, from the breath to digestion, circulation, and even mental and emotional states.

When these pranas are balanced, the mind is calm, clear, and stable. However, imbalances in these vital forces can lead to mental unrest, anxiety, stress, and emotional disturbances. By incorporating mudras, we can work with these pranas to improve mental well-being.

1. Prana Vayu

Prana Vayu is the primary force governing the intake of energy, primarily through breath and sensory experiences. It is located in the chest region and is responsible for respiration and the functioning of the heart and lungs.

Mental Connection: Prana Vayu is linked with clarity, focus, and vitality. When Prana is in balance, the mind feels energized, alert, and capable of handling challenges.

Imbalance: An imbalance in Prana can result in mental fatigue, lack of focus, and feelings of being overwhelmed or scattered.

2. Apana Vayu

Apana Vayu governs the downward and outward movement of energy. It is located in the lower abdomen and is responsible for elimination, reproduction, and grounding energy.

Mental Connection: Apana Vayu is closely tied to emotional stability and the ability to release negative emotions. It helps with grounding the mind and releasing stress, anxiety, and tension.

Imbalance: When Apana is disturbed, one may experience anxiety, fear, and feelings of insecurity. Difficulty in "letting go" of emotional baggage can also arise.

3. Samana Vayu

Samana Vayu is located in the navel area and governs the digestion and assimilation of nutrients. It is the balancing force between Prana and Apana.

Mental Connection: Samana Vayu relates to processing thoughts and emotions, digesting experiences, and bringing balance between mental activity and emotional responses.

Imbalance: An imbalance in Samana Vayu can lead to mental confusion, indecisiveness, and difficulty in managing emotions.

4. Udana Vayu

Udana Vayu is centered in the throat and governs communication, self-expression, and spiritual growth. It moves upward and is associated with voice and speech.

Mental Connection: Udana Vayu governs mental clarity, expression, and emotional upliftment. It helps us express our thoughts and emotions effectively and fosters positive thinking.

Imbalance: When Udana is unbalanced, it can lead to difficulties in communication, lack of confidence, and mental blockages that prevent clear thinking.

5. Vyana Vayu

Vyana Vayu is the all-pervading energy that governs circulation, movement, and the overall distribution of energy throughout the body.

Mental Connection: Vyana supports mental coordination, emotional harmony, and the feeling of being interconnected. It balances both internal and external energy flows, helping to maintain emotional balance and adaptability.

Imbalance: An imbalance in Vyana can lead to a feeling of disconnection, mental restlessness, or the inability to maintain focus during stress.

Mudras to Balance the Pancha Pranas for Mental Health

Mudras can help balance the Pancha Pranas, leading to a harmonious state of mind. By directing the flow of energy, mudras assist in clearing mental blockages and restoring equilibrium to the mind and emotions. Some key mudras for balancing the Pancha Pranas include:

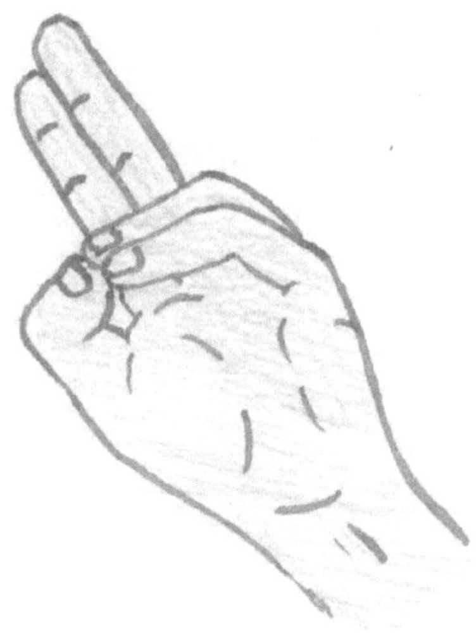

Forming the Prana Mudra:

- Sit comfortably either on the floor or a chair, with your back straight and shoulders relaxed.

- Place your hands on your lap or thighs, palms facing up.

- Touch the tips of your ring finger and little finger (to the tip of your thumb.

- Keep the index and middle fingers extended straight, ensuring a relaxed posture.

Benefits: Prana Mudra enhances vitality and mental focus.

Forming the Apana Mudra:

- Sit comfortably either on the floor or a chair, with your back straight and shoulders relaxed.

- Place your hands on your lap or thighs, palms facing up.

- Touch the tips of your ring finger and middle finger to the tip of your thumb.

- Keep the other two fingers extended straight, maintaining a gentle and relaxed hand position.

Benefits: Apana Mudra releases stress and promotes emotional stability.

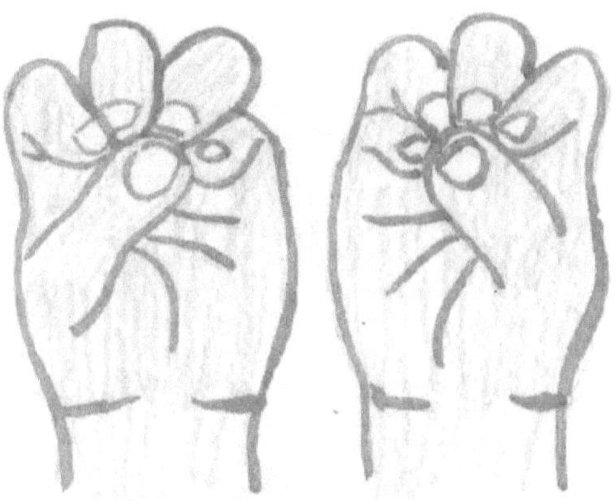

Forming the Samana Mudra:

- Sit comfortably either on the floor or a chair, with your back straight and shoulders relaxed.

- Place your hands on your lap or thighs, palms facing up.

- Bring the tips of all five fingers together on each hand, forming a conical shape.

- Keep the hands relaxed, ensuring the fingers lightly touch without strain.

Benefits: Samana Mudra balances mental energies and aids in digestion.

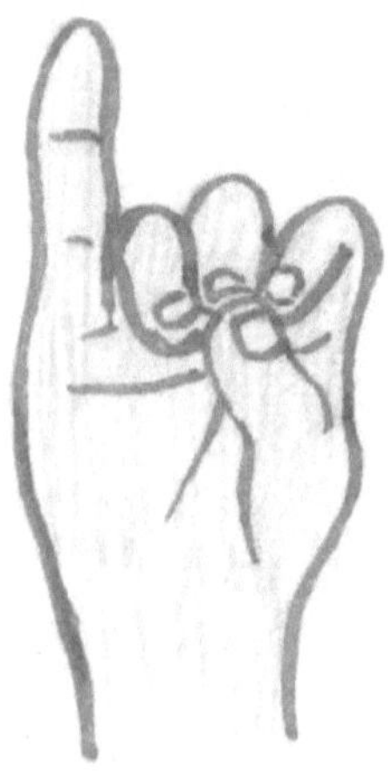

Forming the Udana Mudra:

- Sit comfortably either on the floor or a chair, with your back straight and shoulders relaxed.

- Place your hands on your lap or thighs, palms facing up.

- Touch the tips of your index finger, middle finger, and thumb together, forming a triangle.

- Keep the other two fingers extended straight, maintaining a relaxed posture.

Benefits: Udana Mudra improves self-expression and boosts mental clarity.

Forming the Vyana Mudra:

- Sit comfortably either on the floor or a chair, with your back straight and shoulders relaxed.

- Place your hands on your lap or thighs, palms facing up.

- Touch the tips of your index finger and middle finger to the tip of your thumb.

- Keep the other two fingers extended straight, ensuring your hands remain relaxed.

Benefits: Vyana Mudra supports emotional balance and coordination.

Conclusion:

The Pancha Pranas offer a powerful framework for understanding the deep connection between our mental health and the flow of vital energy within the body. By working with these energies through mudras and other yogic practices, we can bring harmony to the mind and emotions, fostering a sense of inner peace and mental clarity. Through this holistic approach, mental health is not just about managing symptoms but about cultivating a balanced, vibrant, and resilient mind.

THE INTERRELATION BETWEEN GUT AND MENTAL HEALTH

The Role of Gut Microbiota

The gut microbiome is vital for both physical and mental health, influencing digestion, immune function, and the gut-brain connection.

It produces neurotransmitters like serotonin, GABA, and dopamine, which regulate mood and cognition. Remarkably, 90% of the body's serotonin—a key mood regulator—is made in the gut.

Low serotonin levels are linked to depression and anxiety, emphasizing the gut's role in mental well-being.

Symbiotic Relationship with Gut Microbes

Humans and gut microbes share a mutually beneficial relationship:

- **Human Benefits:** The body provides food and shelter for the bacteria.

- **Bacterial Benefits:** The microbes aid digestion, produce vitamins (e.g., biotin, vitamin K), develop the immune system, protect against pathogens, and generate energy for intestinal cells.

When this relationship thrives, so does the human body, much like a well-tended garden.

Dysbiosis: When Balance is Lost

Dysbiosis occurs when gut microbes fall out of balance, disrupting the body's systems. This imbalance is linked to mental health issues like depression, anxiety, and neurodegenerative diseases. A healthy gut is essential to maintaining mental stability and coping with stress.

Gut Health, Nutrient Absorption, and Mood

A healthy gut ensures proper absorption of nutrients vital for brain function, such as vitamins and fats. Deficiencies in these nutrients can affect mood and cognitive health.

Supporting the Gut-Brain Connection

Supporting gut health with a balanced diet and stress reduction can enhance both mental and physical well-being. Achieving harmony in the gut microbiome is a key step toward improving overall health.

बलमारोग्यमायुश्च प्राणाश्चाग्नौ प्रतिष्ठिताः |

अन्नपानेन्धनैश्चाग्निर्ज्वलति व्येति चान्यथा ||३४२||

Strength, health, longevity, and life itself are anchored in the digestive fire, Agni. Charaka Samhita (Sutra

Sthana, Chapter 28, Verse 342) emphasizes that Agni is fuelled by food and drink, and without these, it weakens. Agni is so vital that when it is extinguished, life comes to an end, making it the very foundation, or *mool*, of life. An imbalance in Agni—whether too intense or too weak—can disrupt essential bodily functions, impacting overall well-being.

Agni Mudra ignites the body's digestive fire, reducing the Prithvi (earth) element and increasing the Agni (fire) element. Holding Agni Mudra for a longer period allows one to experience its potency through a noticeable rise in body heat.

Please refer to the chapter on **Pancha Mahabhutas** for the formation and detailed explanation of **Agni/Surya Mudra**.

Benefits: Agni Mudra enhances digestive fire (Jatthar Agni), elevates bloating, improves nutrient absorption and supports gut health by balancing the body's metabolic process.

Pushan Mudra

Pushan Mudra, also known as the "Gesture of Nourishment," is a powerful practice that supports healthy digestion and overall well-being. Symbolizing the natural cycle of receiving, assimilating, and eliminating, it is especially effective when practiced after meals or during times of digestive discomfort. Regular practice can help maintain a balanced digestive system and optimize nutrient absorption.

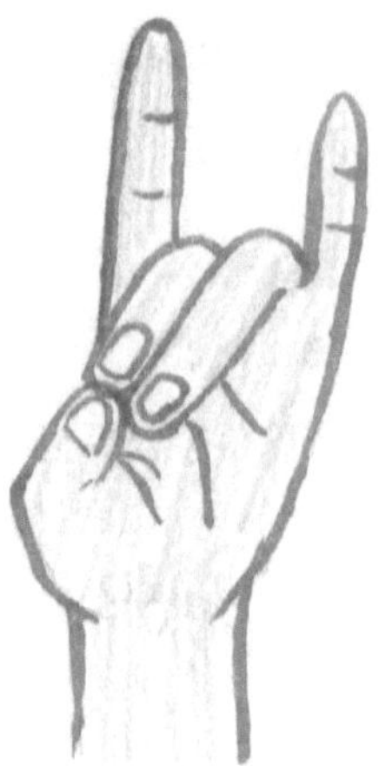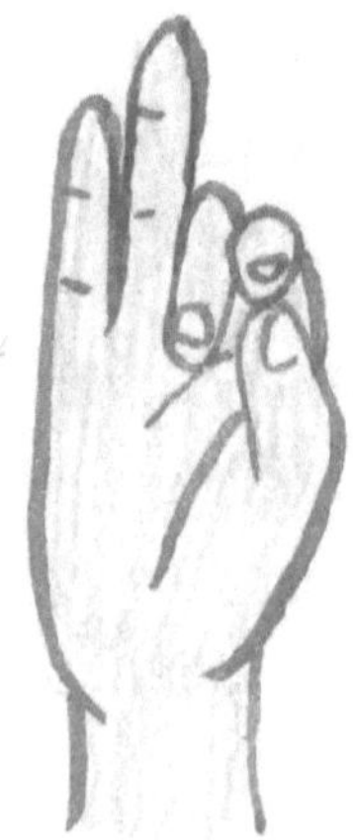

Forming the Mudra:

- Sit comfortably either on the floor or a chair, with your back straight and shoulders relaxed.

- Place your hands on your lap or thighs, palms facing up.

- For the right hand: Touch the tips of the index and middle fingers to the tip of the thumb, while the ring and little fingers remain extended.

- For the left hand: Touch the tip of the middle finger to the tip of the thumb, and extend the index, ring, and little fingers.

- Rest both hands gently on your thighs or knees while seated comfortably.

Benefits: This mudra stimulates digestive organs, relieves bloating and indigestion, promotes elimination, and balances the digestive fire (Jatthar Agni), improving metabolism and enhancing vitality.

Varun Mudra

Varun Mudra, also known as the "Mudra of Water," helps balance the water element in the body, promoting hydration and supporting smooth digestion. This mudra is particularly effective in addressing digestive issues caused by dehydration or dryness in the digestive tract. By promoting hydration, preventing dryness, reducing excess heat, and balancing digestive fire (Agni), Regular practice supports overall digestive comfort and well-being.

Benefits: Varun Mudra aids in relieving constipation, acidity, and sluggish digestion, ensuring a healthy and efficient digestive process.

[Please refer to the chapter on **Panchamahabhutas** for the formation of **Varun/Vayu Mudras.**]

Vayu Mudra

Vayu Mudra, or the "Mudra of Air," helps balance the air element (Vata dosha) in the body, which plays a crucial role in digestion. Excess air in the digestive system can cause issues like bloating, gas, and discomfort. Regular practice supports a balanced flow of air in the body, ensuring digestive ease and maintaining the strength of digestive fire (Jatthar Agni).

Benefits: By practicing Vayu Mudra, one can reduce excess air, promoting smoother digestion and providing relief from these digestive discomforts.

Apana Mudra and Digestion

Apana Mudra is also known as the Mudra of Digestion or the Mudra of Elimination. It plays a crucial role in supporting the body's digestive and detoxification processes.

Please refer to the chapter on **Pancha Pranas** for the formation and detailed explanation of **Apana Mudra**.

Benefits: This mudra helps regulate the downward flow of energy (*Apana Vayu*), which governs the elimination of waste from the body, and improves digestive health.

Conclusion:

The intricate interplay between the gut and the mind reminds us of the profound wisdom in maintaining digestive health for mental well-being. The gut, often referred to as the "second brain," plays a pivotal role in emotional stability, cognitive function, and overall vitality. From producing mood-regulating neurotransmitters to absorbing brain-essential nutrients, the gut microbiome is central to our mental health.

By incorporating practices like Agni Mudra, Pushan Mudra, Varun Mudra, Vayu Mudra, and Apana Mudra, we can actively support our digestive fire (Jatthar Agni) and maintain the delicate balance of the elements within. These mudras, combined with a balanced diet, regular exercise, and stress management, create a holistic approach to gut health.

As emphasized in the Charaka Samhita, the digestive fire is the foundation of life. By nurturing Agni and fostering harmony within our gut microbiota, we not only enhance physical health but also cultivate mental resilience and emotional well-being. In this symbiotic relationship, tending to the gut is a key step toward achieving holistic health and a balanced mind.

MENTAL HEALTH AND ITS RELATION TO THE NERVOUS SYSTEM

Introduction: The nervous system plays a pivotal role in regulating mental health. It acts as the body's communication network, connecting the brain to every organ and function, which includes emotional and mental processes. The relationship between mental health and the nervous system is both intricate and profound, as disturbances in one can directly affect the other.

The Nervous System's Role: The nervous system consists of two main parts:

1. **Central Nervous System (CNS)** – composed of the brain and spinal cord, responsible for processing and interpreting information.

2. **Peripheral Nervous System (PNS)** – connects the CNS to the rest of the body, managing the body's responses to stimuli and maintaining homeostasis.

Mental health issues often stem from imbalances or dysfunctions in this system, influencing how the brain processes emotions, stress, and cognition.

Connection Between Mental Health and the Nervous System

- **Stress and Anxiety**: Stress activates the "fight or flight" response, increasing heart rate and releasing stress hormones. Chronic stress can lead to anxiety and burnout, weakening the body's ability to calm down through the parasympathetic nervous system.

- **Depression**: Imbalances in neurotransmitters like serotonin and dopamine are linked to depression, affecting mood and emotional stability.

- **Neuroplasticity**: Mental health affects neuroplasticity—the brain's ability to adapt. Positive practices like meditation enhance it, while chronic conditions can hinder the brain's recovery from stress or trauma.

- **Autonomic Nervous System (ANS) and Emotions:** The ANS regulates involuntary functions like heartbeat, digestion, and respiratory rate. It has two branches:

  - **Sympathetic Nervous System** (activates fight-or-flight)

  - **Parasympathetic Nervous System** (rest-and-digest)

An imbalance between these systems can lead to emotional disturbances, with an overactive sympathetic response often leading to stress, anxiety, and emotional burnout. Restoring balance through relaxation techniques can calm the nervous system and support mental well-being.

Impact of Mental Health on the Nervous System

Chronic stress keeps the nervous system in a constant state of alert, leading to exhaustion and vulnerability to physical and emotional disorders. Mental health conditions like anxiety, depression, and PTSD disrupt the nervous system, worsening emotional and physical regulation.

Healing the Nervous System with Mudras:

Mudras can soothe and balance the nervous system. By activating specific energy pathways, mudras help calm stress, reduce anxiety, and restore harmony, promoting overall mental and emotional well-being.

Gyan Mudra

Gyan Mudra, also known as the Mudra of Knowledge, is a simple yet powerful gesture that enhances mental clarity, peace, and balance. It is especially beneficial for calming the nervous system, reducing stress, and promoting focus.

Forming the Mudra

- Sit comfortably in a relaxed position, either on the floor or a chair, with your back straight and shoulders relaxed.

- Rest your hands on your knees or thighs, with your palms facing upwards.

- Gently touch the tip of your index finger to the tip of your thumb, forming a circular shape.

- Keep the other three fingers extended and relaxed.

- Close your eyes and take deep, slow breaths, focusing on the sensation of the mudra and the calming energy it brings.

Benefits: This mudra stimulates the brain and helps in the regulation of emotions, creating a sense of calm and mental stability.

Hakini Mudra for Mental Clarity and Nervous System Health

Hakini Mudra is a powerful hand gesture that helps enhance brain function, focus, and mental clarity. It is especially beneficial for calming the nervous system, improving concentration, and reducing stress.

Forming the Mudra

- Sit comfortably in a relaxed position, with your back straight and shoulders relaxed.

- Bring your hands in front of your face, with the palms facing each other.

- Touch the tips of your fingers from both hands to their corresponding fingers (index to index, middle to middle, etc.), leaving the thumbs free to point towards each other.

- Keep your fingers gently touching, forming a pyramid shape with your hands.

- Close your eyes, take slow, deep breaths, and focus on the sensation in your hands, allowing the energy to flow freely between them.

Benefits: This mudra encourages both hemispheres of the brain to work in harmony, promoting emotional balance and mental well-being.

Aakash Mudra is sometimes also called as Shuni Mudra.

[Please refer to the chapter on **Panchamahabhutas** for the formation of **Akash Mudra**.]

Shuni Mudra, also known as the Mudra of Patience, is beneficial for mental focus, emotional stability, and balancing the nervous system.

Benefits: This mudra is particularly effective in enhancing concentration, fostering patience, and helping release negative thoughts or stress, leading to a sense of calm and clarity.

Apana Mudra (Detoxification Mudra)

Apana Mudra, known as the Mudra of Purification, is deeply connected to the element of earth and is highly effective in promoting detoxification and grounding energy.

Benefits: This mudra is known for its ability to soothe the nervous system, reduce stress, and aid in the elimination of toxins, both physically and mentally.

[Please refer to the chapter on **Pancha Pranas** for the formation & detailed explanation of **Prana, Apana Mudras**].

Prana Mudra is a powerful gesture that activates the body's vital energy (Prana), improving vitality, mental clarity, and nervous system function.

Benefits: Prana mudra enhances the flow of energy throughout the body, making it particularly beneficial for reducing fatigue, improving focus, and supporting emotional well-being.

Conclusion: The nervous system and mental health are deeply interconnected. Maintaining a balanced nervous system is essential for emotional well-being, and taking care of one's mental health, in turn, keeps the nervous system functioning optimally. Understanding this relationship helps in better managing mental health and improving overall quality of life.

By incorporating practices like Prana Mudra, Apana Mudra, Gyan Mudra, Vayu Mudra, Akash Mudra, and Hakini Mudra, we can soothe and balance the nervous system. The mudras mentioned above activate specific energy pathways, alleviate stress, reduce anxiety, and restore inner harmony, thereby fostering overall mental and emotional well-being.

Impact of Mental Health on the Heart

Poor mental health often leads to unhealthy coping mechanisms like smoking, overeating, or inactivity, which negatively impact heart health. Stress activates the "fight-or-flight" response, elevating heart rate and blood pressure, weakening the heart muscle, and increasing the risk of heart disease. Anxiety can cause palpitations, chest pain, and shortness of breath, with panic attacks mimicking heart attack symptoms, adding ongoing strain on the heart. Research also shows that depression and chronic stress heighten the risk of heart attacks and strokes due to prolonged stress hormone exposure, increased inflammation, and unhealthy habits.

Healing the Heart Through Mental Wellness:

Yoga techniques such as asanas, meditation, mindfulness, and mudras reduce stress and enhance heart health by improving mental well-being and boosting mood-regulating neurotransmitters. These practices activate the parasympathetic nervous system, promoting relaxation, lowering heart rate, and reducing blood pressure. The vagus nerve, a vital component of this system, plays a key role in regulating both heart rate and emotional responses, fostering holistic well-being.

Mudras can support vagus nerve activation by promoting relaxation, calming the nervous system, and enhancing parasympathetic activity. Below are some mudras that can assist in activating the vagus nerve:

Dvimukham Mudra

This mudra promotes a sense of calm, enabling you to let go of immediate stress and connect with your inner wisdom. It gently transitions the nervous system into relaxation mode, activating the parasympathetic response for deep peace.

Forming the Mudra:

- Sit comfortably either on the floor or a chair, with your back straight and shoulders relaxed.

- Place your hands in front of your chest with palms facing forward.

- Bring the tips of your thumb and index fingers together on both hands to form a circular shape.

- Position the other fingers extended straight and slightly apart, creating a two-faced appearance.

- Keep your hands relaxed while maintaining this gesture.

Benefits: By enhancing the downward flow of energy and breath (apana vayu), this mudra fosters tranquility, helping to lower blood pressure and alleviate stress.

Adi Mudra

Adi Mudra, signals the body to slow down, reduce stress, and enter a state of calm. It helps lower heart rate, decrease tension, and promote overall well-being. Perfect for moments of stress or before meditation, Adi Mudra helps in centering your energy and reconnecting with a sense of inner peace. It helps activate a subtle but powerful energy flow that specifically nurtures the parasympathetic nervous system.

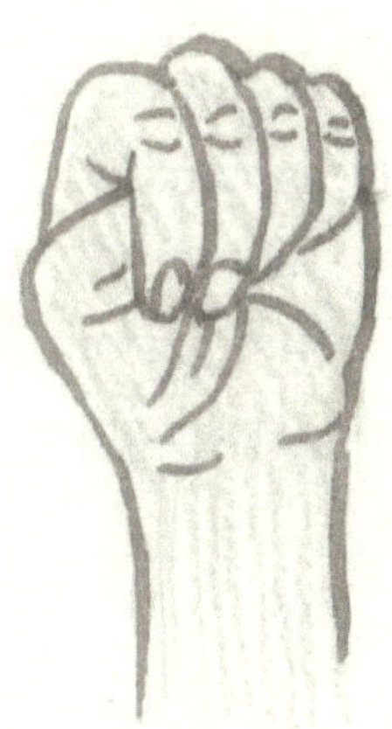

Forming the Mudra:

- Sit comfortably either on the floor or a chair, with your back straight and shoulders relaxed.

- Place your hands on your lap or thighs, palms facing up.

- Fold your thumbs inward to touch the base of your little fingers.

- Curl the remaining fingers gently over your thumbs to form a fist.

- Keep your hands relaxed while maintaining this position.

Benefits: This mudra encourages the body to move out of the fight-or-flight mode and into a peaceful, healing state.

Brahmi/Brahma Mudra

Brahmi Mudra, stimulates the calming energies within, reducing stress, anxiety, and mental fatigue. Perfect for moments of mental strain, Brahmi Mudra provides soothing relief, grounding the mind and facilitating relaxation, to experience greater clarity, peace, and balance.

Forming the Mudra:

Instead of knees when the folded hands of Adi Mudra are placed close to the navel (Manipura Chakra (Solar Plexus)), with the folded knuckles facing up it becomes Brahmi Mudra.

Benefits: It encourages the body to shift from a state of heightened alertness to a place of restfulness, allowing the parasympathetic nervous system to take charge.

Apana Vayu Mudra (Gesture of the Heart)

Apana Vayu Mudra, also known as the Heart Mudra or Mrita Sanjeevani Mudra, is a powerful hand gesture to support heart health. For those, who often deal with high stress and long hours, practicing Apana Vayu Mudra can be a valuable tool for maintaining a healthy heart and reducing hypertension.

Forming the Mudra:

- Sit comfortably either on the floor or a chair, with your back straight and shoulders relaxed.

- Place your hands on your lap or thighs, palms facing up.

- Touch the tips of your thumb, middle finger, and ring finger together.

- Bend your index finger to touch the base of your thumb.

- Keep the little finger extended.

- Rest your hands on your knees with palms facing upward.

Benefits: This mudra is particularly effective in balancing the body's energy and promoting cardiovascular well-being.

Conclusion: The relationship between mental health and the cardiac system is complex and interconnected. Maintaining mental well-being is crucial for heart health, and vice versa. Understanding this connection can help individuals make lifestyle changes that protect both their mental and cardiac health, leading to a balanced and healthier life.

By incorporating practices like Dvimukham Mudra, Adi Mudra, Brahmi Mudra, and ApanaVayu Mudra, we can maintain both mental well-being as well as heart health.

The mudras mentioned above activate the parasympathetic nervous system, promoting relaxation, lowering heart rate, and reducing blood pressure. The vagus nerve, a vital component of this system, plays a key role in regulating both heart rate and emotional responses, fostering holistic well-being.

Connection Between Mental Health and the Skeletal System

Mental health and the skeletal system may seem unrelated at first glance, but there is a significant connection between the two. Mental well-being plays a crucial role in maintaining overall health, including the health of bones and joints.

Likewise, problems within the skeletal system can influence mental health, highlighting the intricate relationship between mind and body.

The skeletal system gives the body structure, protects organs, enables movement with muscles, and stores vital minerals like calcium and phosphorus. Healthy bones are key to mobility and overall vitality.

Impact of Mental Health on Bones and skeletal Health:

Stress/Anxiety and Bone Health:

Chronic stress raises cortisol levels, which can weaken bone density by hindering bone formation and increasing bone loss, raising the risk of osteoporosis.

Stress also disrupts calcium absorption, essential for strong bones, leading to weaker bones and higher fracture risk.

Depression and Bone Health:

Depression increases the risk of osteoporosis due to higher inflammatory markers that harm bone health. It also impacts lifestyle habits like reduced activity, poor nutrition, smoking, and alcohol use, weakening bones and skeletal strength.

Impact of Bone Problems on Mental Health:

Chronic Pain and Depression: Individuals suffering from bone-related conditions like arthritis, osteoporosis, or fractures often experience chronic pain. This constant discomfort can lead to mental health issues, including depression, anxiety, and stress, as pain interferes with daily life and limits mobility.

Fatigue and Mood Swings: Bone and joint pain, particularly when persistent, can result in fatigue and irritability, affecting mood and emotional stability. In turn, negative emotional states can exacerbate the perception of pain, creating a vicious cycle between mental health and physical discomfort.

Posture and Mental Health: Mental health affects posture, which is closely tied to skeletal alignment. Stress or depression often contribute to slouching or poor posture, straining bones, joints, and muscles, and causing musculoskeletal pain. Conversely, improving posture can alleviate skeletal discomfort and enhance mental well-being.

To balance mental and bone health, the following mudras can be highly beneficial:

Sandhi Mudra: A Remedy for Joint Pain and Flexibility

This Mudra combines the qualities of **Prithvi Mudra** (right hand) and **Akash Mudra** (left hand), creating a powerful fusion that helps balance the Vata dosha, which governs the flexible movement of the joints.

It also helps repair joint injuries from exercise or overuse, restores energy, and enhances movement. Helps in chronic joint pain, improving flexibility and reducing discomfort.

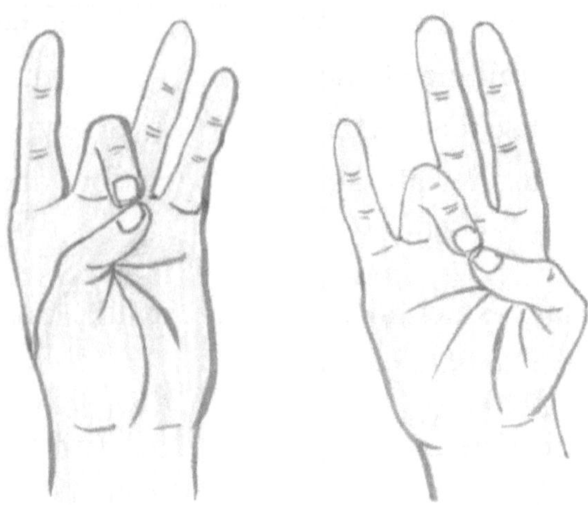

Forming the Mudra:

- Sit comfortably in a relaxed position, either on the floor or a chair, with your back straight and shoulders relaxed.

- Rest your hands on your knees or thighs, with your palms facing upwards.

- With your right hand, form **Prithvi Mudra** by touching the tip of your ring finger to the tip of your thumb, keeping the other fingers extended.

- With your left hand, form **Akash Mudra** by touching the tip of your middle finger to the tip of your thumb, keeping the other fingers extended.

- Gently press the tips of the fingers in both hands together, forming a balanced connection between the right and left hands.

- Close your eyes, take deep, slow breaths, and focus on the sensation of the mudra, allowing the energy to flow and relieve any tension in your joints.

Benefits: It is particularly effective in alleviating knee pain, stiffness, and discomfort by restoring energy and addressing the lack of the space element in the joints.

Merudanda Mudra

It is a simple yet powerful hand gesture designed to address back pain and support spinal health. By positioning the fingers of both hands in a specific posture, this mudra activates nerve points that connect to the spine, helping to relieve pain and promote healing.

The subtle energy released through these finger points interacts with the affected areas of the back, charging the energy and releasing negative blockages.

Forming the Mudra

- Sit comfortably in a relaxed position, either on the floor or a chair, with your back straight and shoulders relaxed.

- Rest your hands on your knees or thighs, with your palms facing upwards.

- With your right hand fold your little finger and middle finger towards the thumb

- touch the tips of both fingers to the tip of the thumb.
  With your left hand fold your index finger towards the thumb.

- Place the tip of the index finger on the middle part of the thumb.

Benefits: This mudra soothes the spinal cord, improving the overall functioning of the nervous system and helps relieve muscle cramps caused by overuse or strain.

Vata Nashak Mudra

Vata Nashak Mudra is a powerful hand gesture designed to balance the Vata dosha, which governs the elements of air and space in the body. This mudra helps regulate prana, reducing the excess Vata that causes discomfort and pain. Additionally, it boosts stamina and endurance, making it an excellent practice for overall vitality.

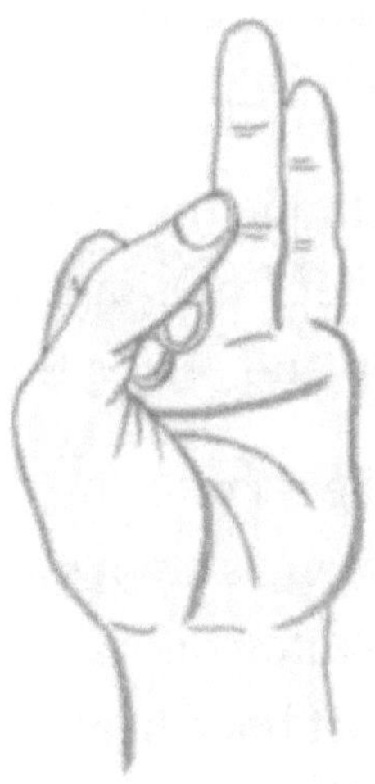

Forming the Mudra:

- Sit comfortably in a relaxed position, either on the floor or a chair, with your back straight and shoulders relaxed.

- Rest your hands on your knees or thighs, with your palms facing upwards.

- With your right hand, touch the tip of your thumb to the tip of your index finger, forming a circular shape, and extend the other fingers gently.

- With your left hand, touch the tip of your thumb to the tip of your middle finger, also forming a circular shape, and extend the other fingers gently.

- Keep both hands relaxed and placed comfortably on your knees or thighs.

Benefits: By calming the air and ether elements, this Mudra provides relief from joint pain and constipation, improving digestion and easing flatulence.

Conclusion: The relationship between mental health and the skeletal system is a powerful example of how the mind and body are interconnected. Mental health issues can negatively impact bone health, while problems in the skeletal system can lead to mental health challenges. By addressing both, individuals can support overall well-being, ensuring that both the body's structural foundation and emotional balance are maintained.

By incorporating practices like Sandhi Mudra, Merudanda Mudra, and Vatanashak Mudra, we can balance mental and bone health.

Relationship Between Body Weight, Body Image, And Mental Health

Introduction

The relationship between body weight, body image, and mental health is profound and multifaceted. Our body type and weight not only influence our physical health but also significantly impact our emotional well-being, self-esteem, & social interactions.

Understanding this connection is essential for fostering holistic health.

Mental Health's Influence on Weight

- **Stress and Emotional Eating**: Stress triggers the release of cortisol, which can lead to overeating or cravings for unhealthy foods. This contributes to weight gain, creating a cycle of stress and dissatisfaction.

- **Eating Disorders:** Condition such as anorexia nervosa, bulimia nervosa, and binge-eating disorder—are not just about food; they reflect deeper struggles with self-image, control, and emotional well-being.

- **Depression and Weight Fluctuations**: Depression can lead to weight gain due to inactivity or emotional eating, or weight loss due to appetite suppression, affecting both physical and emotional health.

- **Anxiety's Role**: Anxiety can cause a loss of appetite or reliance on "comfort foods," resulting in unhealthy weight changes.

The Impact of Body Type and Weight on Mental Health

- **Body Image Concerns**: Unrealistic societal standards of beauty often create pressure to conform to certain body types, leading to dissatisfaction with one's body. This dissatisfaction can manifest as low self-esteem, anxiety, or depression.

- **Weight Stigma and Discrimination**: People with higher or lower body weights often face stigma, which can result in social isolation, stress, and negative self-perception, compounding mental health challenges.

Cultivating a Positive Body Image

- **Self-Acceptance Practices**: Emphasizing body positivity and self-compassion can improve mental health, regardless of weight or body type.

- **Mindfulness and Gratitude**: Techniques like mindful eating and gratitude for the body's capabilities foster a healthier relationship with oneself.

Mudras for Weight Gain:

Aditi Mudra

Aditi Mudra, inspired by ancient Vedic hymns, is closely associated with the earth element, which is believed to be symbolized by Aditi, the name given to the earth in Vedic texts.

This mudra specifically targets the ring finger, the seat of the earth element, and when gently pressed by the thumb, it helps balance the earth energy within the body. This dual action of the earth and fire elements promotes physical health, contributing to weight management and overall fitness.

Forming the Mudra:

- Sit comfortably either on the floor or a chair, with your back straight and shoulders relaxed.

- Place your hands on your lap or thighs, palms facing up.

- Raise both hands simultaneously to chest height, keeping the movements fluid and mindful.

- Gently press the base of your ring finger with the pad of your thumb.

- Allow the other fingers—index, middle, and little— to extend naturally, keeping them relaxed.

Benefits: Regular practice of Aditi Mudra detoxifies the body by eliminating waste and toxins, while also enhancing the fire element, which improves digestion and regulates metabolism.

Shakti Mudra

Shakti Mudra, named after the goddess Shakti—an embodiment of feminine energy, creativity, and power—represents dynamic strength and vitality. Often associated with Goddess Durga, this mudra is a symbol of inner resilience and balance. Also known as Shakti Chalana Mudra, where "Chalana" means "movement" or "flow" in Sanskrit, this gesture is designed to enhance the flow of life-force energy (prana) throughout the body. By harmonizing this energy, Shakti Mudra supports vitality, boosts the immune system, and fosters a sense of stability and well-being.

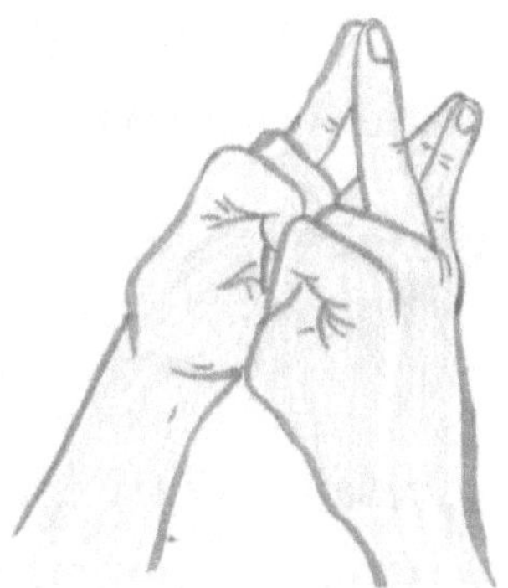

Forming the Mudra:

- Sit comfortably either on the floor or a chair, with your back straight and shoulders relaxed.

- Place your hands on your lap or thighs, palms facing up.

- Raise both hands simultaneously to chest height with smooth and mindful movements.

- Fold the thumbs into the palms of each hand.

- Curl the ring fingers and little fingers to touch the tips of the thumbs gently.

- Extend the index and middle fingers outward, keeping them relaxed and slightly apart.

- Hold the mudra at chest height or rest your hands gently on your thighs with palms facing upward.

Benefits: It is particularly effective in alleviating general weakness, promoting overall health, and aligning the body with its natural rhythms.

Mudras for Weight Loss:

Linga Mudra

Linga Mudra represents the triumph of positive energy over negativity, serving as a powerful tool to ignite the body's inner fire. This activation generates revitalizing energy that supports the proper functioning of internal organs. By stimulating the digestive system, this mudra encourages a harmonious energy flow, aiding in the resolution of gut-related concerns. Its capacity to increase internal heat further contributes to metabolic efficiency, promoting vitality and well-being.

Forming the Mudra:

- Sit comfortably either on the floor or a chair, with your back straight and shoulders relaxed.

- Place your hands on your lap or thighs, palms facing up.

- Raise both hands simultaneously to chest height with smooth and mindful movements.

- Interlock the fingers of both hands, keeping them clasped firmly.

- Ensure that the thumb of one hand is upright and encircled by the thumb and index finger of the other hand.

- Hold the mudra at chest height.

Benefits: This mudra is known to boost metabolism, making it an effective practice for weight management and enhancing overall digestive health.

Kapha-Nashak Mudra

Kapha-Nashak Mudra is a powerful practice for managing weight and improving overall health. By practicing this mudra regularly, especially in the morning, you can support your body's natural processes, promote weight loss, and enhance overall well-being.

Forming the Mudra:

- Sit comfortably either on the floor or a chair, with your back straight and shoulders relaxed.

- Place your hands on your lap or thighs, palms facing up.

- Bend the ring finger and the little finger towards the palm.

- Now, join them with your thumb.

- Put as much pressure as you are comfortable with.

- Practice this mudra for 30-45 minutes every day.

Benefits: Particularly effective for conditions like obesity, hypertension, and indigestion, this mudra works by harmonizing the body's pH levels. Balanced pH levels are crucial for maintaining a healthy metabolism and preventing weight gain.

Mukula Mudra for Balancing and Maintaining Weight:

Mukula Mudra, also known as Samana Vayu mudra (the prana that governs digestion and metabolism), is a powerful gesture that harmonizes the body's energy, especially in the digestive and metabolic systems. When practiced with mindfulness, it can also assist in promoting balance, both physically and energetically, in terms of body weight management.

To balance mental energies and aid in digestion.

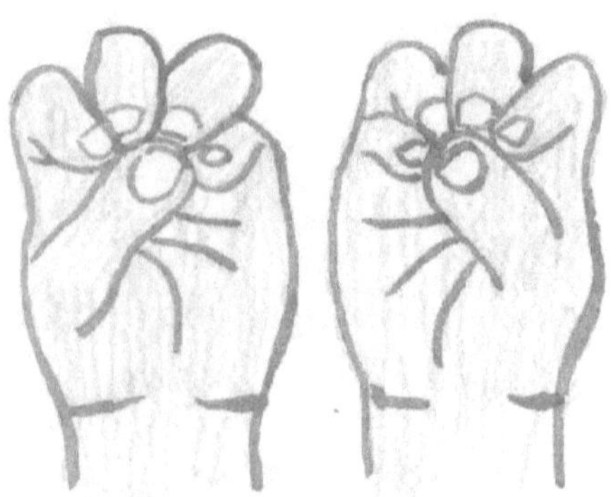

Forming the Mudra:

- Sit comfortably either on the floor or a chair, with your back straight and shoulders relaxed.

- Place your hands on your lap or thighs, palms facing up.

- Bring the tips of all five fingers together on each hand, forming a conical shape.

- Keep the hands relaxed, ensuring the fingers lightly touch without strain.

Benefits: This mudra creates a balanced flow of energy within the body, contributing to overall well-being.

Conclusion

The interplay between weight, body type, and mental health is complex but manageable with a balanced approach. By understanding this connection and integrating holistic practices like mindful eating,

Yogasanas, mudras and meditation, individuals can nurture both their body and mind.

Incorporating practices like Aditi Mudra and Shakti Mudra helps alleviate general weakness, promote overall health, maintain a healthy body weight, and align the body with its natural rhythms.

Linga Mudra, Kapha-Nashak Mudra, and Mukula Mudra facilitate a harmonious flow of energy within the body, promoting balanced pH levels essential for a healthy metabolism. These practices support weight management and enhance overall well-being.

Disclaimer

The information provided in this book on mudras for mental health is intended to complement, not replace, professional medical advice or treatment. While mudras can support mental well-being, they are not a substitute for diagnosis, treatment, or medication prescribed by a qualified healthcare professional.

If you are currently receiving treatment for mental health conditions do not stop or change any medication or treatment plan without the guidance of your healthcare provider. Mudras are meant to enhance your mental health journey, working alongside conventional methods to promote overall wellness.

About the Author

Shilpa Mehta: *A Journey of Yoga and Lifelong Learning*

Shilpa Mehta embarked on her Yoga journey in 1996, immersing herself in the true essence of Yoga at an ashram. Her practice deepened through training at esteemed institutions such as The Yoga Institute, Kaivalya Dham, Shri Ambika Yoga Kutir, and Mumbai University. During this period, she also taught Kathak dance and pre-primary classes, showcasing her versatility as an educator.

An avid reader, traveler, and YouTuber, Shilpa began sharing her Yoga expertise in 1998. Over the years, she has conducted various health camps for professionals, including doctors, executives, chartered accountants, and teachers. Originally focusing on physical platform, Shilpa now extends her teachings online, reaching a global audience.

Shilpa has also coordinated teacher training courses at The Yoga Institute for more than a decade. Holding a master's degree in philosophy and having studied positive psychology, she brings a deep intellectual and emotional understanding to her practice. Additionally, she has served as a speaker and judge at international Yoga conferences.

Currently, Shilpa teaches Yoga at Dhirubhai Ambani International School and has been dedicated to her craft for over 21 years. Her passion for Yoga not only ignites her purpose in life but also fulfills it through both practice and teaching.

May I Ask You For A Small Favor?

At the outset, I want to thank you for reading this book. You could have chosen any other book, but you took mine, and I appreciate this.

I hope you got at least a few actionable insights that will positively impact your day-to-day life.

Can I ask for 30 seconds more of your time?

I'd love it if you could leave a review of the book. That will help me grow my readership by encouraging folks to take a chance on my books.

Keeping it straight - reviews are the lifeblood of any author.

It will take less than a minute of your time but will help me reach out to more people.

If you enjoyed this book, I would greatly appreciate it if you could leave an honest review where you purchased it. I'd love to read your thoughts. Thank you for your support!

Mudras For Teachers: *Enhance Voice Clarity, Cultivate Emotional Resilience, Boost Classroom Presence, and Empower Teaching With Hand Gestures*

Mudras and Meditation for Chakra Healing : *Boost Your Energy, Reduce Stress, Find Clarity, and Experience a Lasting Sense of Inner Peace*

www.ingramcontent.com/pod-product-compliance
Lightning Source LLC
Chambersburg PA
CBHW020625160726
47991CB00002BA/933